Countries Around the World

Costa Rica

Elizabeth Raum

www.raintreepublishers.co.uk
Visit our website to find out more information about Raintree books.

To order:
☎ Phone 0845 6044371
🖷 Fax +44 (0) 1865 312263
🖳 Email myorders@raintreepublishers.co.uk

Customers from outside the UK please telephone +44 1865 312262

Raintree is an imprint of Capstone Global Library Limited, a company incorporated in England and Wales having its registered office at 7 Pilgrim Street, London, EC4V 6LB – Registered company number: 6695582

Edited by Louise Galpine and Megan Cotugno
Designed by Ryan Frieson
Original illustrations © Capstone Global Library, Ltd, 2012
Illustrated by Oxford Designers & Illustrators
Picture research by Tracy Cummins
Originated by Capstone Global Library, Ltd
Printed in China by China Translation and Printing Services

ISBN 978 1 406 22787 1 (hardback)
15 14 13 12 11
10 9 8 7 6 5 4 3 2 1

ISBN 978 1 406 22816 8 (paperback)
16 15 14 13 12
10 9 8 7 6 5 4 3 2 1

British Library Cataloguing in Publication Data
Raum, Elizabeth.
Costa Rica. -- (Countries around the world)
972.8'6052-dc22
A full catalogue record for this book is avail[able from the]
British Library.

Acknowledgements
We would like to thank the following for permission to reproduce photographs: © Alamy: p. 32 (© Thornton Cohen); © Corbis: pp. 7 (© Chris Cheadle/All Canada Photos), 8 (© JUAN CARLOS ULATE/Reuters), 21 (© Kevin Schafer); © Getty Images: pp. 9 (Bob Stefko), 15 (Chris Cheadle), 23 (ELMER MARTINEZ/AFP), 27 (Andy Nelson/The Christian Science Monitor), 29 (Gustavo Caballero/WireImage for NARAS), 31 (Scott Barbour), 39 (Andy Nelson/The Christian Science Monitor); © Imageworks: p. 34 (© David Frazier); © istockphoto: pp. 11 (© Martin Harrison), 17 (© Stephen Meese), 25 (© Focus_on_Nature); © Shutterstock: pp. 5 (© Tony Northrup), 16 (© TranceDrumer), 18 (© worldswildlifewonders), 19 (© Matthew W Keefe), 28 (© Steve Cukrov), 35 (© worldswildlifewonders), 38 (© Timur Kulgarin), 46 (© c.); © SuperStock: pp. 13 (© age footstock), 30 (© Lonely Planet).

Cover photograph reproduced with permission of Corbis/ © Jim Zuckerman.

We would like to thank Richard Abisla for his invaluable help in the preparation of this book.

Every effort has been made to contact copyright holders of any material reproduced in this book. Any omissions will be rectified in subsequent printings if notice is given to the publisher.

Disclaimer
All the Internet addresses (URLs) given in this book were valid at the time of going to press. However, due to the dynamic nature of the Internet, some addresses may have changed, or sites may have changed or ceased to exist since publication. While the author and publisher regret any inconvenience this may cause readers, no responsibility for any such changes can be accepted by either the author or the publisher.

Contents

Some words in the book are in bold, **like this**. You can find out what they mean by looking in the glossary.

Introducing Costa Rica

Have you ever been to Costa Rica? Thousands of tourists visit this **tropical** paradise every year. Costa Rica is located in Central America, and forms a bridge between North and South America. Costa Rica, which covers 51,100 square kilometres (19,730 square miles), is more than twice the size of Wales.

Peaceful people

Most of Costa Rica's 4.5 million people live in the Central Valley where San José, the capital and largest city, is located. The people, who call themselves *ticos*, are proud that Costa Rica is a peaceful nation. Costa Rica is one of only 18 countries in the world that has no standing armies (permanent military force).

Beaches and volcanoes

Costa Rica has over 1,290 kilometres (800 miles) of coastline. Rugged mountain ranges, which include over 100 volcanoes, separate the coastal areas. **Rainforests** and **cloud forests** attract tourists to Costa Rica. Today, tourism is Costa Rica's largest industry. Tourists enjoy surfing in coastal waters, rafting on rivers, and hiking through rainforests.

A paradise for plants and animals

Costa Rica has an amazing variety of plant and animal **species**. It is home to over 9,000 species of plants, 2,000 species of butterflies, and 876 species of birds. Giant turtles, poisonous snakes, jaguars, and various kinds of monkeys add to the country's **biodiversity**. Costa Rica's national parks and nature reserves help to preserve the wildlife.

Costa Rica's Arenal volcano is one of the ten most active volcanoes in the world.

History: seeking peace

People have been living in Costa Rica for over 10,000 years. Early people moved from place to place hunting and gathering food. Sometime between 8000 and 4000 BC, they established villages. Farming developed between 4000 and 1000 BC. Forests covered 90 per cent of the land. Early people burned forests for space to plant crops. They grew corn, fruit trees, and root plants, such as **cassava**.

Native peoples lived in village groups under a chieftain. They fought to gain land, goods, and slaves. They traded with distant groups for products such as cotton, shells, dyes, and artwork. They even traded colourful bird feathers for Mexican gold.

In 1940 United Fruit Company workers found several round stone balls near the Térraba River. Some were the size of golf balls. Others weighed over 16 tonnes. Ancient people probably made these balls between AD 600 and 1500 by hammering and grinding large round boulders until they were perfectly round. No one knows the original purpose of the stone balls.

The Spanish arrive

Christopher Columbus reached Costa Rica in 1502. When he saw natives wearing gold jewellery, he wrote letters to Spain claiming he had discovered gold. He was wrong. There was no gold in Costa Rica.

About 400,000 native people lived in Costa Rica when Columbus arrived. Some fled into the forests and remote valleys. Others were captured as slaves, and many more died of diseases brought from Europe.

Decrease of Costa Rica's native population

Year	Indigenous population
1502	400,000
1569	120,000
1611	10,000
1700	1,300

Source: 2002 census CIA

Costa Rica is a country in Central America, bordered by Nicaragua and Panama.

Ancient Costa Rican people created these giant stone balls.

"Rich coast"

In 1522 Spaniard Gil González Dávila named the land Costa Rica, which means "rich coast." Like Columbus, he expected to find gold. Instead, the Spanish settlers became farmers growing wheat and tobacco. Spanish priests built churches, and **converted** the native people to the **Catholic** religion. Today, nearly all of Costa Ricans speak Spanish and most are Catholics.

Students carry Costa Rican flags on 15 September, Independence Day.

Ethnic background

Today, most Costa Ricans are white or **mestizo** (people with both European and Native American ancestors). People from Jamaica (listed as Black) and China immigrated to Costa Rica in the late 1800s to work on banana plantations or to build railroads.

Ethnic Background	Percentage
White or *Mestizo*	94
Black	3
Native American	1
Chinese	1
Other	1

Independence

In 1821 Spain granted independence to all of its Central American **colonies**, including Costa Rica. The first head of state, Juan Mora Fernández, took office in 1824. He declared San José the capital. Throughout the 1800s, a series of strong **dictators** ruled Costa Rica. They gained power by using force. However, in 1889 Costa Rica became a **democracy**. For the first time, the people truly elected their own leader.

JUAN SANTAMARÍA
(1831–1856)

In 1856 Juan Santamaría became a national hero when he helped defeat an army from Nicaragua. He ran towards the building where enemy troops were hiding and set it on fire. The troops shot at Santamaría, and he died of his wounds on 11 April. But his brave action saved the Costa Rican troops. Today, 11 April is a national holiday honouring Juan Santamaría.

National flag and emblem

In 1848 Costa Rica adopted its flag and **emblem**. The Costa Rican flag (see page 46) has five horizontal stripes in blue, white, and red with the national seal in the centre. The words *"República de Costa Rica"* surround the national seal.

Coffee brings changes

In the 1800s, Costa Ricans began growing coffee beans. By the 1840s, Costa Rica was sending high quality coffee beans overseas. The economy boomed. So did the population. It increased from about 100,000 in 1850 to 250,000 by 1900. The cities grew, too, and there was more entertainment available, such as ice rinks, circuses, and bullfights.

Civil war

In 1940, Rafael Ángel Calderón Guardia became president of Costa Rica. Calderón worked to improve conditions for workers by establishing a minimum wage, **unemployment benefits**, and paid holidays. He also founded the University of Costa Rica.

But when he sought re-election in 1948, he lost. His defeat led to a civil war between Calderón's supporters and followers of José María ("Don Pepe") Figueres Ferrer. Don Pepe, who was supported by the governments of Guatemala and Cuba, seized the cities of Cartago and Puerto Limón. Calderón gave in before Don Pepe could take over the capital city, San José. The war lasted 40 days. About 2,000 people died.

Don Pepe became one of Costa Rica's most important leaders. He extended voting rights to women and black people. Under his leadership, Costa Ricans adopted a new **constitution** and abolished the army.

Bringing peace

In the 1980s, a civil war in neighbouring Nicaragua spilled over into Costa Rica. President Óscar Arias Sánchez developed a peace plan to stop the war. He was awarded the **Nobel Peace Prize** in 1987 for his efforts.

Today, over 4.5 million people live and work in Costa Rica. In 2010 Laura Chinchilla, the first female president, took office.

In Costa Rica, coffee is grown on large **plantations** like this one.

Regions and resources: something for everyone

Scientists think that 80 million years ago, Costa Rica was a series of volcanic islands. Gradually, the islands formed a land bridge between the continents of North and South America with the Pacific Ocean on the west and the Caribbean Sea on the east.

Climate

Costa Rica has two seasons: rainy and dry. The rainy season extends from May to late November. The dry season lasts from December through to April. The average temperature in Costa Rica is between 22 and 27 °Celsius (71 and 81 °Fahrenheit). March and April are warmest.

This map shows the land height and major natural features of Costa Rica.

San José is located in the Central Valley.

The Central Valley

Most *ticos* live in the Central Valley. The cities of San José, Alajeula, Cartago, and Heredia are located here. In these cities, wealthy people live in large homes or apartments. Most workers live in one-storey homes of concrete blocks or wood. The poor often live in **shantytowns**. Coffee is grown on large **plantations** as well as on smaller farms throughout the Central Valley.

The mountains

Two mountain regions cross Costa Rica: the Cordillera Volcánica and the Cordillera de Talamanca. They include many volcanoes. Many mountain peaks are over 3,600 metres (12,000 feet) high. Arenal, the most active volcano, has erupted almost every day since 1968. There hasn't been a major eruption of Irazú, the largest volcano, since 1965.

Earthquakes are also common in Costa Rica. On 20 May 2010, an earthquake struck 64 kilometres (40 miles) from San José. It was felt as far away as Panama, but did not cause major damage.

How to say...

coffee bean	*el grano de café*	ehl GRAH-no deh kah-FEH
corn	*el maíz*	ehl mah-EES
pepper	*el pimiento*	ehl pee-mee-EN-to

The Northwest

The **province** of Guanacaste was originally covered by tropical forests. The forests were cut down in the 1950s to allow for cattle ranching. Today, Guanacaste is sometimes called Costa Rica's "Wild West". Ranching is big business and **rodeos** are popular.

Coastal plains

Costa Rica has nearly 1,290 kilometres (800 miles) of beaches along its coasts. On the Pacific coast, fishing is an important industry. Tuna and shrimp are the most valuable commercial fish. Most are shipped to the United States. The coastal plains are hot, swampy, and heavily forested. Bananas grow well. Pineapples are the second most important crop. Sugarcane, tropical fruits, and **cacao** (used to make chocolate) grow here. Other forest products include rubber, chicle (used to make chewing gum), plants used for medicine, and woods such as balsa and mahogany.

Costa Rica **imports** more goods and raw materials than it **exports** to other countries.

	Imports	Exports
Goods	raw materials, consumer goods, petroleum, construction materials	bananas, pineapples, coffee, melons, ornamental plants, sugar, beef, seafood, electronic components, medical equipment
Major trading partners	United States, Mexico, Venezuela, Japan, China	United States, Netherlands, China, Mexico
Total value	£6.81 billion (2009 est.)	£5.543 billion (2009 est.)

Other industries

In addition to agriculture, new industries are thriving in Costa Rica. Companies are producing computer equipment, medical equipment, fabric, clothing, construction materials, **fertilizer**, and plastic products.

Human resources

Costa Rica's fertile land, frequent rainfall, and many people are its most important resources. The **national anthem**, written in 1903, honours Costa Rica's hard-working farmers. It ends with a wish that no one will bother the contented and peaceful people of Costa Rica as they continue their labours.

Costa Rican National Anthem

"Himno Nacional de Costa Rica"

Noble homeland, your beautiful flag
Expression of your life it gives us:
Under the limpid blue of your skies,
Peace reigns, white and pure.
In the tenacious battle of fruitful toil,
That brings a glow to men's faces,
Your sons, simple farm hands
Gained eternal renown, esteem, and honour,
Gained eternal renown, esteem, and honour.
Hail, gentle country!
Hail, loving mother!
If anyone should attempt to besmirch your glory,
You will see your people, valiant and virile,
Exchange their rustic tools for weapons.
Hail, O homeland! Your prodigal soil
Gives us sweet sustenance and shelter.
Under the limpid blue of your sky,
May peaceful labour ever continue!

Wildlife: amazing variety

Costa Rica has an amazing variety of wildlife. Its varied landforms – mountain ranges, rainforests, and coasts – attract different **species**. Thousands of years ago, a land bridge allowed animals to **migrate** through on their way between North and South America. Many species stayed in the area.

Birds and butterflies

Costa Rica's rainforests are home to 18 per cent of the world's butterfly species. Costa Rica also has several farms that raise butterflies. The eggs are shipped to butterfly houses all over the world. Costa Rica is among the top 20 most **biodiverse** nations.

Birds	Insects	Mammals	Reptiles	Amphibians	Plants
876 species	34,000 species	205 species	220 species	160 species	9,000 species

The blue morpho is one of the largest butterflies in the world.

Costa Rican wildlife laws protect jaguars.

Of Costa Rica's 876 bird species, more than 630 live there all year round. The rest spend winters in Costa Rica and fly north in summer. Birdwatchers come to Costa Rica from all over the world to see birds such as the attila, who eat frogs whole after bashing them against trees, or the brightly coloured toucans, who pick fruit from trees. Birds of prey, such as eagles and ospreys, soar through the treetops. Tiny hummingbirds flit through the rainforest beating their wings up to 100 times per second.

The jaguar corridor

Jaguars slink through Costa Rican forests searching for food. Farmers have learned to make room for the big cats. The government set aside areas as jaguar corridors, or protected trails, that jaguars use to pass from one area to another. Although jaguars sometimes eat livestock, they leave people alone.

Deadly creatures

The poison dart frog is one of many deadly creatures that live in Costa Rica. Two kinds of crocodiles lurk in muddy rivers along the Caribbean coast. Boa constrictors – long, fat snakes up to about 3 metres (10 feet) long – crush their victims to death. The bite of the fer-de-lance snake can kill, but snakebite deaths are rare in Costa Rica.

Poison dart frogs have a chemical in their skin that can paralyze larger animals.

How to say...

butterfly	*la mariposa*	lah mah-ree-PO-sah
snake	*la serpiente*	lah ser-pee-EN-tay
turtle	*la tortuga*	lah tor-TOO-gah

Scary, but not deadly

Other reptiles, such as the fierce-looking iguana, are harmless to humans. Anteaters use long, sticky tongues to eat from anthills. Four types of monkey leap from tree to tree in the rainforests. The collared peccary, a piglike mammal, is a vegetarian. The coati, with the ringed tail and masked face of a raccoon, eats fruits and small animals.

Strange creatures

The brown-throated three-toed sloth (see page 35) lives in rainforests. It sleeps for up to 20 hours at a time and protects itself with its sharp claws. The common basilisk is a small iguana that can run up to 101 metres (331 feet) on the surface of water.

Sea creatures

Large sea mammals, such as the manatee and the humpback whale, live in the warm **tropical** waters off Costa Rica's coast. Four of the world's seven species of turtle nest on the beaches. **Environmentalists** work to protect turtles. Turtles often get caught in nets set by shrimp fisherman. Sometimes they die when they swallow plastic bottles which they mistake for jellyfish.

Ostional National Wildlife Refuge is one of the most important nesting areas for Olive Ridley sea turtles.

Tourism

Tourists from all over the world come to Costa Rica. The beaches and mountains offer outdoor adventure. The national parks and preserves allow tourists to observe Costa Rican plants and animals. In the northwest, tourists ride horses along Pacific beaches and visit working farms. Visitors to San José enjoy visiting churches, markets, and art museums. Tourism is Costa Rica's largest industry.

Eco-tourism is travel to natural areas that preserve the environment. Visitors take photographs, but try not to harm the many plants and animals of the rainforests, **cloud forests**, or beaches. Young Costa Ricans often work in the national parks and reserves providing services to eco-tourists.

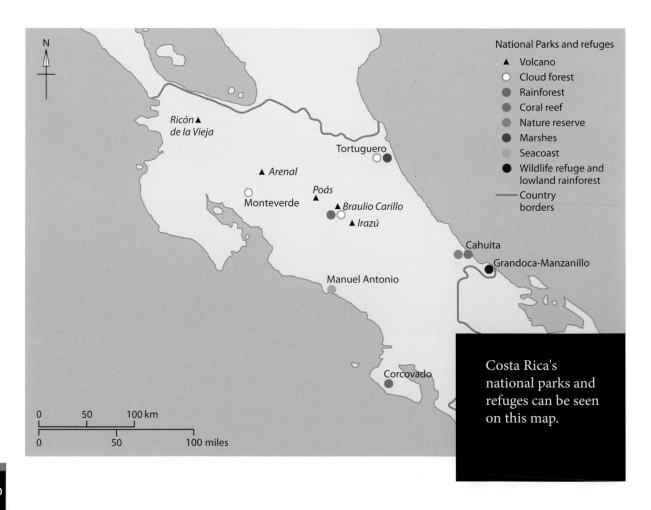

Costa Rica's national parks and refuges can be seen on this map.

Rainforests, volcanoes, and cloud forests

In coastal areas, rainforests attract visitors who enjoy hiking through the jungle or rafting. Tourists can walk along bridges suspended from trees to see birds, animals, and reptiles. It is possible to visit active volcanoes, climb into a **dormant crater**, or visit a cloud forest. Cloud forests, such as the Monteverde Cloud Forest Preserve, are high-altitude rainforests where clouds settle on the mountain tops.

YOUNG PEOPLE

Adventure tourism also attracts young people to Costa Rica. Surfing, mountain biking, white water rafting, snorkelling, and mountain climbing are popular with teenagers and young adults. Costa Rica, with its volcanoes, rushing rivers, and beautiful beaches, offers wild adventures to visitors.

Adventure tourists enjoy rafting on the Pacuare River in Costa Rica.

Infrastructure:
a constitutional republic

Costa Rica is a **democratic** republic. The people elect their leaders. According to the 1949 **constitution**, all citizens are equal under the law. Citizens have the right to vote in national elections, own property, and speak freely.

Three branches

The national government is divided into three branches. The Executive Branch includes the president, two vice presidents, and a cabinet of advisers. The Legislative (law-making) Branch is made up of the 57 elected members of the Legislative Assembly, called *diputados*. The Judicial Branch is the court system. Elections are held every four years.

This map shows Costa Rica's seven provinces.

Costa Rica has seven provinces, but they do not have any power to make or change laws. The president appoints governors for the provinces. Decisions are made by the national government, not by the provinces.

Daily life

Costa Ricans are very polite. They greet one another with a handshake or a kiss on the cheek.

LAURA CHINCHILLA (BORN 1959)

Costa Rica's first woman president, Laura Chinchilla, took office in May 2010. She held several offices in the government before running for president. She served as minister of public security. Later, she served as vice president and justice minister. She promised to increase spending for education and law enforcement.

Providing help for everyone

Costa Ricans are proud of the services provided by the government. Electric power and telephone service is available almost everywhere despite the difficulties in remote, mountainous areas. A government agency makes sure that all people have clean drinking water.

Government programmes also provide healthcare. Almost everyone is covered by health insurance. There are 10 major hospitals in Costa Rica, as well as smaller clinics throughout the country. **The World Health Organization** ranks Costa Rica's healthcare system 36 out of 190 nations.

Becoming green

In June of 2007, President Óscar Arias, pledged that by 2021, Costa's Rica's 200th birthday, the nation would become green, or **carbon neutral**. This means that Costa Rica will use **renewable** energy sources such as water, wind, and solar energy, rather than fossil fuels such as oil and gas. Because of the mild climate, most homes do not need heating.

Costa Rica is making good progress toward this goal. By 2010, 99.2 per cent of Costa Rica's energy came from renewable sources. The government has built 12 large **hydroelectric** power plants on Costa Rica's rivers to provide electricity. A large wind farm was built in Guanacaste in 2002. Others are being built in the mountains of Escazú and Santa Ana.

Volcano power

Costa Rica is even using volcanoes for energy. **Geothermal** plants use hot steam from deep inside the volcanoes to provide electricity. Two plants will begin operating in 2011 near Rincón de la Vieja Volcano in Guanacaste.

Tourists can walk along this hanging bridge in the Monteverde Cloud Forest.

Education

Costa Rica has the highest **literacy rate** in Central America. About 96 per cent of all Costa Ricans over 15 can read and write. School is required from kindergarten to year 10. About 65 per cent of students finish secondary school. Students must pass tests to move from one year to the next.

Daily life

In Costa Rica, the school day is from 7.00 AM to between 1.00 and 4.00 PM. Pupils wear uniforms and bring their own lunches. They study Spanish, maths, social studies, science, English, and computer sciences. Children attend school from mid-February to mid-December with a few weeks off in July.

Preparing for the future

English classes have been required in Costa Rican schools since 1994. President Figueres ordered all 4,000 schools in Costa Rica to teach English and to provide computers for student use. He wanted to prepare young people to work in the tourist industry and with new **technology**.

The University of Costa Rica in San José is Costa Rica's oldest and largest university. It has 35,000 students. In 2010 it cost £125 per semester to attend. Costa Rica has 38 other universities and colleges.

FRANKLIN CHANG-DÌAZ (BORN 1950)

Franklin Chang-Dìaz, born in San José, is an engineer, scientist, and astronaut. Dìaz, a citizen of both Costa Rica and the United States, made a world record seven space flights from 1981 to 2005. He believes that Central America can play a major role in science and space technology. He is currently leading a Costa Rican programme called "21st Century Strategy," designed to improve life in Costa Rica.

How to say...

school	*la escuela*	lah es-kway-la
book	*el libro*	ehl LEE-bro
pencil	*la lapiz*	lah LA-pees

Children in Costa Rica wear uniforms to school.

Culture: celebrating life

Most Costa Ricans follow the Christian religion. About 76.3 per cent are **Catholic**. Another 15.7 per cent follow the **Protestant** faith.

Holidays

Most Christian holidays are official holidays in Costa Rica. *Ticos* also celebrate Independence Day and Juan Santamaría Day (see page 9). Fireworks, street parties, and parades mark New Year's Day and other national holidays.

Museums, theatres, and music

The brightly decorated wooden ox-carts, often seen in holiday parades, are a national symbol. In the 1800s, teams of oxen pulled carts full of coffee beans on a 10- to 15-day journey from the coffee fields to the Pacific coast. The Ox-cart Museum in San José has several ox-carts on display.

Brightly decorated ox-carts, called *carretas*, are recognized throughout the world as a symbol of Costa Rica.

Ticos enjoy going to movies and the theatre. Costa Rica has an international film festival and an international music festival. Monteverde holds a yearly music festival that lasts for six weeks. *Ticos* enjoy a wide range of music, from classical to folk and rock.

DEBI NOVA (BORN 1980)

Pop singer Debi Nova was born in San José. Aged 14, she sang with Gandhi, a Costa Rican rock band. At 17, she moved to the United States and performed with many well-known artists including the Black-Eyed Peas and Ricky Martin. Her 2010 album *Luna Nueva* (New Moon) includes songs in both Spanish and English. She describes Costa Rica as "a very peaceful place . . . I grew up listening to various types of music from around the region."

Fútbol

Football, or *fútbol*, is the most popular sport in Costa Rica. Young *ticos* attending school in the United Kingdom in the early 1900s brought the sport back to Costa Rica. By 1921 Costa Rica had established a National Football League. Today, there are many regional teams that compete against one another. The national team plays in large stadiums in San José, but in small towns, people gather in the plazas to watch their teams challenge one another. Even the smallest village has a football pitch.

Children and teenagers practice their football skills all year long.

Radio and television

Costa Rica has 116 radio stations and 20 television stations. One TV station is government-owned. Most Costa Ricans get their news from television. More than 90 per cent of homes have a television set.

Ticos watch an average of 6.4 hours of TV a day. This is about twice as much as people in the United Kingdom. Young *ticos* enjoy watching *fútbol* matches on TV. Soap operas called *novelas* are also popular. Many American TV programmes are available in Spanish.

Women's roles

Most household tasks, including childcare, are done by women in Costa Rica. However, women also work outside the home. Many have college or university educations and hold jobs as teachers, nurses, in business, or in government.

Costa Rica has taken steps to include women in government. Election rules require that 40 per cent of candidates for political office must be women. In 2010 Costa Ricans elected a woman president and 22 female members of the Legislative Assembly.

Daily life

Whether they are rich or poor, Costa Ricans value family life. Often children, parents, and grandparents live together in one house. Grandparents help to prepare meals and care for the children while the parents work.

Eat like a *tico*

Rice and beans is the standard dish in Costa Rica. *Ticos* may add fish, meat, or eggs to their rice and beans, but often they eat it plain. Roast pork is the most popular meat. Fish is available near the coasts. Costa Ricans serve salads of fresh cabbage, tomatoes, and carrots. Corn is used in tortillas or corn pancakes.

In Costa Rica, lunch is the big meal of the day. Even so, it is not a large meal. Costa Rican portions are smaller than in Europe or the United States. *Ticos* rarely eat dairy products. They prefer fresh fruits like papaya, mango, pineapple, watermelon, and cantaloupe.

Gallo Pinto is a rice and black bean dish eaten for breakfast throughout Costa Rica. Its name means "spotted rooster."

Gallo Pinto

Gallo Pinto (Spotted Rooster) is an easy to make dish. It is eaten for breakfast, lunch, or dinner. This recipe makes 6 servings. Ask an adult to help you, especially when using the hot stove.

Ingredients:

- 700 grams freshly cooked rice
- 470 grams freshly cooked black beans
- 2 tablespoons onion, finely chopped
- 1 tablespoon green pepper, finely chopped
- 2 tablespoons coriander, finely chopped
- Salt and pepper to taste
- 2 tablespoons oil
- ½ tablespoon Worcestershire Sauce
- ½ tablespoon Tabasco Sauce (optional)

Preparation:

Heat up the oil in a saucepan or frying pan. Add onion and pepper. When they are lightly browned, add the beans and cook for 2 more minutes. Add the rice and mix well, cook for another 3 minutes. Add the Worcester sauce, Tabasco Sauce and the chopped coriander. Mix well and cook for another minute. Serve with salsa.

Costa Rica today

A recent American study named Costa Rica the fifth cleanest nation in the world. Only Switzerland, Norway, Sweden, and Finland ranked higher. Costa Rica earned its high rating based on its clean water, use of clean energy, and **biodiversity**.

Welcoming to visitors

Costa Rica is a safe and welcoming place. Tourists come to enjoy Costa Rica's biodiversity and to explore the rainforests, **cloud forests**, volcanoes, and seashores. Over half of Costa Rica's workers are employed by the tourist industry, and tourism is increasing.

These *tico* teenagers reflect different backgrounds. The boy on the left is descended from Jamaican immigrants. The one on the right has Spanish ancestors.

The brown-throated three-toed sloth is one of Costa Rica's many amazing mammals.

Some **environmentalists** worry that as tourism grows, it will harm the environment. While large hotels may bring more money to the country, some block beautiful views and increase **pollution**. That's why the Costa Rican government encourages the building of small hotels. Currently 80 per cent of Costa Rica's hotels have 20 or fewer rooms.

A model for others

The people of Costa Rica tend to stay in their homeland. Few move elsewhere. After all, Costa Rica has good education and health systems, stable government, and satisfactory housing. Costa Rica has much to teach the world. It is a peaceful place, and its education and medical services are among the best in Central America. Leaders around the world are looking to Costa Rica as a model nation.

Fact file

Official name: Republic of Costa Rica

Nationality: Costa Rican

Location: Central America (considered part of both North and South America)

Capital: San José

Largest cities: San José (population 356,200)
Limón (population 65,600)
Alajuela (population 51,000)

Land area: 51,100 square kilometres (19,730 square miles)

Bordering countries: Nicaragua to the north, Panama to the south

System of government: Democratic Republic

Army: Abolished in 1949

Date of independence: 5 September 1821 (from Spain)

Date of constitution: 7 November 1949

Climate: tropical and subtropical; dry season (December to April); rainy season (May to November); cooler in highlands

Coastline: 1,290 kilometres (800 miles)

Major rivers: the Chirripa, Frío, General, San Juan, and Tempisque

Major volcanoes: Irazú, Arenal, and Poas

Highest point: Cerro Chirripo – 3,810 metres (12,500 feet)

Lowest point: Pacific Ocean (sea level) – 0 metres (0 feet)

Terrain: a rugged, central range separates the eastern and western coastal plains

Natural resources: hydroelectric power, geothermal power, forest products, and fisheries products

Local currency: Colón (named after Christopher Columbus)

Agriculture products: bananas, pineapples, coffee, beef, sugar, rice, dairy products, vegetables, fruits, ornamental plants, corn, beans, potatoes, timber

Major industries: tourism, electronic components, medical equipment, textiles and clothing, tyres, food processing, construction materials, fertilizer, plastic products

Exports: integrated circuits, medical equipment, bananas, pineapples, coffee, melons, ornamental plants, sugar, textiles, electronic components

Major markets: United States 32.6%, Netherlands 12.8%, China 11.8%, and Mexico 4.2%

Imports: raw materials, consumer goods, petroleum

Major suppliers: United States 44.7%, Mexico 7.65%, Venezuela 5.56%, China 5.15%, and Japan 4.36%

Population:	4,509,290 million
Languages:	Spanish (official), English
Life expectancy:	77.7 years
Literacy rate:	96%
Official religion:	Roman Catholic, but there is freedom to practice others
National anthem:	"Himno Nacional de Costa Rica"

Costa Rica is home to many beautiful birds and flowers such as this hummingbird and these orchids.

National tree:	Guanacaste tree
National flower:	Guaria Morada
National bird:	Yigüirro
National symbol of work:	Costa Rican ox-cart

National holidays:

1 January	New Year's Day
March or April	Holy Week
11 April	Juan Santamaría Day
1 May	Labour Day
25 July	Annexation of Guanacaste Day
2 August	Patron Saint Day – Virgin of Los Angeles
15 August	Mother's Day and Assumption
15 September	Independence Day
2 November	All Soul's Day
25 December	Christmas Day

Famous Costa Ricans:

Francisco Amighetti (1907–1998), painter
Rafael Angel Calderón Guardia (1900–1970), president who gave workers rights
Laura Chinchilla (born 1959), first female president
Franklin Chang-Dìaz (born 1950), astronaut and scientist
Juan Mora Fernández (1784–1854), first head of state
José María ("Don Pepe") Figueres Ferrer (1906–1990), president who adopted a new constitution
Claudia Poll (born 1972), Olympic swimmer
Silvia Poll (born 1970), Olympic swimmer
Óscar Arias Sánchez (born 1940), president who won the Nobel Peace Prize for his efforts to bring peace to Central America
Juan Santamaría (1831–1856), national hero

Timeline

BC is short for "before Christ". BC is added after a date and means that the date occurred before the birth of Jesus Christ, for example, 450 BC.

AD is short for *Anno Domini*, which is Latin for "in the year of our Lord". AD is added before a date and means that the date occurred after the birth of Jesus Christ, for example, AD 720.

12,000–8,000 BC	People begin to settle in the area that is Costa Rica
8,000–4,000 BC	Early people establish villages
4,000–1,000 BC	First farming begins in the area
AD 600–1500	Térraba River stone balls are thought to made at some point during this period
1502	Christopher Columbus visits the area; Europeans name it Costa Rica
1523	Spanish establish their first settlement on the Pacific coast
1540	Costa Rica becomes part of **New Spain**
1561	Spain's Juan de Cavallón leads first Spanish colonists to Costa Rica
1736	City of San José is founded
1791	Coffee plants introduced to Costa Rica
1821	Central America gains independence from Spain
1823	Costa Rica joins the United Provinces of Central America
1838	Costa Rica gains independence
1874	Banana cultivation begins

1949	New constitution adopted, giving women and people of African descent the right to vote
1949	Costa Rican army abolished
1963–65	Irazú volcano erupts, causing serious damage to agriculture
1968	Arenal volcano erupts, causing many casualties
1971	National Park system is established
1982	Costa Rica comes under US pressure to oppose the Sandinist National Liberation Front, a socialist political party in Nicaragua
1985	US-trained force begins operating in Costa Rica
1987	President Óscar Arias Sánchez wins the Nobel Peace Prize
1997	Tourism replaces coffee as top industry
2007	Costa Rica announces that it will become first voluntarily "carbon neutral" country
2010	Laura Chinchilla becomes first female president

Glossary

biodiversity variety of different species living within a certain area

cacao bean of a small tropical tree that is the source of cocoa

carbon neutral adding no extra carbon dioxide to the environment, in order to reduce climate change

cassava root plant used as food

Catholic Christian church headed by the pope

cloud forest high-altitude rainforest where mist is almost always present

colony territory in a new land with ties to the home state

constitution system of laws and principles that govern a nation, state, or corporation

convert convince someone to adopt a different religion

crater depression in the Earth that marks the opening of a volcano

democracy form of government in which the power lies with the people

dictator ruler with absolute power over people

dormant not currently active

emblem sign, design, or figure that represents something

environmentalist someone who works to protect the air, water, animals, plants, and other natural resources from pollution or its effects

export ship goods or materials to other countries or places for sale or exchange

fertilizer substance used to make the soil richer and help plants grow

geothermal energy from heat deep inside the Earth

hydroelectric type of electricity that is produced by moving water

import bring products or workers in from a foreign country for use, sale, or services

literacy rate number of adults over the age of 15 who can read and write

mestizo person who has both European and native ancestors

migrate pass from one region to another

national anthem song officially adopted by a country

New Spain former name for Spanish territories in the Western Hemisphere, including many South American and Latin American countries

Nobel Peace Prize annual international award funded by money left by the Swedish industrialist, Alfred Nobel

plantation large area used for agriculture, usually with resident workers

pollution introduction of harmful substances and products into the environment

Protestant Christian religion that does not recognize the authority of the pope

province administrative division of a country

renewable able to be replaced over time

rodeo public exhibition of cowboy skills, such as bronco riding and calf roping

shantytown section of a city or town with crudely built houses and shelters

species class of living creatures that look similar and can breed with one another

technology knowledge dealing with computers, engineering, or applied science

tropical hot and humid

unemployment benefits money paid to an unemployed worker by the government during a period of unemployment.

World Health Organization agency body of the United Nations that works to improve and promote world health

Find out more

Books

Costa Rica, Erin Foley and Barbara Cooke (Benchmark, 2008)

Costa Rica (Country Explorers), Tracey West (Lerner, 2009)

Costa Rica (Central America Today), Charles Shields (Mason Crest Publishers, 2009)

Rainforests (100 Facts), Camilla de la Bedoyere (Miles Kelly, 2009)

The Vanishing Rainforest, Richard Platt (Frances Lincoln, 2006)

Websites

kids.nationalgeographic.com/kids/places/find/costa-rica
Find out some more fascinating facts about Costa Rica.

www.costarica-homeschool.com
Discover more about the animals that live in the rainforests of Costa Rica.

www.factmonster.com/ipka/A0934201.html
To learn about kids in Costa Rica, visit the Factmonster website.

www.timeforkids.com/TFK/teachers/aw/wr/main/0,28132, 1597311,00.html
Go on a sightseeing tour of Costa Rica!

www.costaricatraveller.com/about_costa_rica/national_anthem.htm
You can hear Costa Rica's national anthem at this website.

www.visitcostarica.com/ict/paginas/home.asp?idioma=2
Visit Costa Rica's Official Tourism Institute.

Places to visit

If you are ever lucky enough to travel to Costa Rica, here are some fascinating places you can visit:

Arenal Volcano
www.arenal.net

Corcovado National Park
www.corcovado.org

Monteverde Cloud Forest Reserve
www.monteverdeinfo.com/monteverde.htm

Rincón de la Vieja Volcano National Park
www.costarica-nationalparks.com/rincondelaviejanationalpark.html

Santa Rosa National Park
www.costaricabureau.com/nationalparks/santarosa.htm

Topic tools

You can use these topic tools for your school projects. Trace the map onto a sheet of paper, using the thick black outlines to guide you.

Adopted in 1848, the flag is formed by five horizontal stripes: the first and the fifth are blue, the second and the fourth are white, and in the middle there is a red stripe double the width of each of the other four stripes. The national emblem was adopted in 1848. The seven stars forming an arch represent the seven provinces of the republic. Copy the flag design and then colour in your picture. Make sure you use the right colours!

■ San José

N

Index